Kitchen Renovation

Dr. WADE

Table of Contents

Summary 4

Preface 6

Prologue 8

Forward 10

Chapter No. 1 12

   Embarking on Your Kitchen Renovation Adventure 12

Chapter No. 2 16

   Setting Your Renovation Goals: Defining Your Vision 16

Chapter No. 3 19

   Budgeting for Success: Financial Planning for Your Dream Kitchen....19

Chapter No. 4 23

   Exploring Kitchen Design Styles: From Traditional to Modern..........23

Chapter No. 5 27

   Crafting a Functional Layout: Maximizing Space Efficiency 27

Chapter No. 6 31

   Storage Solutions: Organizing Your Kitchen Space....................31

Chapter No. 7 35

   Countertop Considerations: Choosing the Perfect Surface................35

Chapter No. 8 39

Chapter No. 9 45

Cinks and Faucets: Functional Features with Design Impact 45

Chapter No. 10 50

Kitchen Appliances Unveiled: From Essentials to Innovations............50

Chapter No. 11 55

Lighting Your Kitchen: Creating Ambiance and Functionality 55

Chapter No. 12 60

Flooring Foundations: Durability and Design underfoot 60

Chapter No. 13 64

Backsplash Brilliance: Elevating Your Kitchen Walls............................64

Chapter No. 14 68

Harmonizing Colors: Designing a Cohesive Kitchen Palette 68

Chapter No. 15 72

Eco-Friendly Choices: Sustainable Options for Your Renovation 72

Chapter No. 16 76

Navigating Plumbing and Electrical Upgrades....................................76

Chapter No. 17 80

Working with Professionals: Contractors and Designers 80

Chapter No. 18 85

DIY vs. Professional Renovation: Pros and Cons 85

Chapter No. 19 88

Permits and Building Codes: Navigating Legal Requirements............88

Chapter No. 20 91

Preparing for Renovation: Demolition and Site Readiness 91

Summary

"Dream Kitchen Renovation: A Comprehensive Guide" is a comprehensive guide that guides the reader through the complex process of remodeling a kitchen space. From concept to completion, this book provides valuable information, practical tips and expert advice to help you make your remodel a success.

Based on the importance of clear goals, readers are guided to define the goals of renovation – be it to improve functionality, improve aesthetics or both. The book emphasizes the need to set a realistic budget that meets these goals and ensures a balanced approach that doesn't strain your finances.

The book looks at different cooking styles with examples to help readers understand how each style contributes to the overall picture. The practical implications of these styles on layout and functionality have been explored, helping readers make informed choices that match their vision.

The functional design of the kitchen is fundamental and the book explains its importance in detail. Through ergonomic design principles and sophisticated storage solutions, readers learn how to optimize their space for stress-free everyday activities.

materials such as counters and cabinets are studied in detail and their characteristics and properties are determined. This gives readers the opportunity to select materials that balance aesthetics with durability and maintenance considerations.

appliances, the heart of every kitchen, deserve special attention. The reader is informed about the latest developments and possibilities for saving energy and can thus make decisions that combine design requirements with practical needs.

The book also looks at lighting and flooring, providing an overview of their impact on the environment and functionality. With a focus on sustainability, readers are empowered to make environmentally conscious choices that make a positive impact.

The book acknowledges the expertise of professionals and offers advice on choosing reputable contractors and designers. Compliance with local building codes and permits is also highlighted as a crucial step.

The book ends with an appreciation of the end result and advice on how to keep the charm and functionality of a renovated kitchen. Armed with new knowledge and insights into future trends, readers can confidently and creatively embark on a journey of renewal.

Essentially, Dream Kitchen Renovation: A Comprehensive Guide is an indispensable companion for anyone tackling a kitchen renovation. With careful guidance and expert advice, the book debunks the complex process and enables readers to transform the kitchen into a beautiful and functional space.

Preface

Welcome to Revitalize Your Kitchen: a journey into the space of your dreams. This book is a comprehensive guide into the world of kitchen renovation, a space where creativity, function and design come together to create a culinary paradise tailored to your individual tastes and needs.

A kitchen remodel is more than just a DIY project; It's an opportunity to transform one of the most central and valuable areas of your home. Whether you're a seasoned DIY enthusiast or just starting out with the remodel, this book is designed to give you the knowledge, ideas, and inspiration you need to confidently embark on this exciting journey.

In the following chapters, we'll look at all aspects of a kitchen renovation, from conceptualizing your vision to the final design detail. We learn the art of setting clear goals that reflect your lifestyle and ambitions, giving you a solid foundation for future decisions. A realistic budget is the basis of a successful renovation and we will help you to balance your dreams with your financial resources.

The heart of your kitchen is its design and layout. Our exploration of different styles will help you find an aesthetic that suits you. Then we delve into the science of functionality and share insights into creating a space that optimizes workflow and storage efficiency.

materials, appliances, lighting, flooring and green options play a key role in a successful renovation. Within these pages you'll find expert advice to help you make decisions that enhance both the beauty and practicality of your kitchen.

We also understand the importance of expertise and will guide you in selecting the right contractors and designers who can bring your ideas to life. Navigating permits and regulations can be daunting, but we provide you with the information you need to ensure a smooth and compliant renovation process.

As you leaf through these pages, imagine the transformation that awaits your kitchen. Let this book be your trusted guide through every decision, challenge, and victory. Whether you're looking for a subtle modernization or a total makeover, Bring Your Kitchen to Life can help you on your journey to the kitchen of your dreams.

Prologue

The Kitchen: A place where culinary magic unfolds, families gather and memories are made. It's a piece that holds a special place in our hearts and homes, but often longs to be rejuvenated. Welcome to Kitchen Rebirth: Creating Your Own Culinary Oasis, a journey into the art of transforming that essential space into an oasis of functionality and beauty.

Renovating a kitchen isn't just limited to replacing worktops or applying a new coat of paint. It is a company that combines creativity, practicality and personal expression. As we journey together, let us explore the myriad choices, challenges, and joys that await.

On the following pages you will find a comprehensive guide to all aspects of kitchen renovation. We dive deep into the process of creating a vision for your dream kitchen, defining your goals and setting a budget that sets the stage for an incremental transformation. From contemporary elegance to rustic charm, we explore a variety of design styles that reflect your unique taste and lifestyle.

Your kitchen layout is the canvas on which the renovation masterpiece is painted. Our exploration of design principles will help you create a space that is both aesthetically pleasing and intuitively functional. Storage solutions, an important part of any kitchen, are removed to keep your newly renovated kitchen clean and tidy.

materials and finishes are textures and colors that bring your vision to life. We will explore the possibilities of countertops, cabinets and floors and provide insights into their properties and contribution to aesthetics. In the gadgets section, we look at the latest innovations that combine practicality and efficiency.

From atmospheric lighting to elaborate rear walls, we will show you how details can improve the ambience of your kitchen. Additionally, our exploration of green choices will empower you to make sustainable choices that leave a positive footprint.

In the pursuit of perfection in the kitchen, we value the role of professionals who turn dreams into reality. We'll help you select experts who share your vision and handle the necessary logistics for permits and codes.

As you leaf through these pages, imagine the rebirth of your kitchen. This book is your companion, offering advice, inspiration, and a roadmap to meeting your challenges. Whether your renovation is a personal project or a family affair, Kitchen Revival is here to inspire you and prepare you for this exciting journey of transformation.

Forward

When you embark on your kitchen renovation journey, you strive to transform the centerpiece of your home. If you're holding Remodel Your Kitchen: A Guide to Creating a Culinary Sanctuary; You're not just holding a book in your hands—you're holding a plan to create a space that seamlessly blends functionality and beauty.

The kitchen is more than a room; It's a place of creativity, connectivity and comfort. Here, the smell of freshly prepared food mixes with laughter and conversation. Memories are burned into every corner. And now that you're on the brink of renewal, this book is your trusty companion.

These pages have many resources to guide you through each phase of the renovation process. From the first spark of an idea to the final bloom of the backsplash, we've curated handpicked ideas, tips, and inspiration to empower you.

Your journey of renewal begins with clear intentions. Process, budget and desired results all work together to create the kitchen rug of your dreams. We accompany you in these early decisions and help you to identify opportunities and align your goals.

The project is a place where imagination takes shape. We explore the spectrum of styles, from classic to contemporary, rustic to elegant, and explore how each choice shapes the character of your kitchen. With special attention to the layout of the space, we will discover the secrets of space optimization and an efficient workflow to make working in the kitchen a pleasure.

The materials become the cornerstones of your project. Countertops, cabinetry and flooring are explained, helping you choose pieces that complement your aesthetic while meeting the demands of everyday living.

devices are tools for culinary discovery. We navigate a sea of options, helping you find the perfect balance of technology, practicality, and design coherence.

Digging deeper, we examine sustainable lighting, color schemes and choices that integrate sustainability into your renovation story. We'll give you the knowledge you need to connect with professionals who can turn your vision into reality and guide you through the intricacies of permits and regulations.

Together we invent, design and create a kitchen that reflects your personality, suits your lifestyle and contains the essence of what a kitchen should be. From "Renovate Your Kitchen"; You're not just renovating the space—you're creating a sanctuary where the memories will stay alive for years to come. Let's take this adventure step by step and turn your kitchen into a canvas of culinary delights and home harmony.

Chapter No. 1

Embarking on Your Kitchen Renovation Adventure

Introduction

A kitchen remodel is an exciting and transformative journey that can enhance both the functionality and aesthetics of your home. The kitchen, the heart of the home, serves as a meeting point, a culinary sanctuary and a center of creativity. Whether you're a seasoned do-it-yourselfer or prefer the help of a pro, careful planning and thoughtful decision-making are key to a successful kitchen remodel. This comprehensive guide will walk you through all steps of the process, helping you overcome your challenges and maximize the benefits of your kitchen remodel.

1. Set Goals and Budget

Before you begin any remodeling project, it's important to set a clear set of goals. Looking to create a more spacious room layout, upgrade your devices, upgrade your storage solutions, or get a whole new aesthetic? In addition to setting goals, setting a realistic budget is essential. Consider all expenses, including materials, labor, permits, and potential contingencies to ensure your vision stays within budget.

2. Research and inspiration

Dive into the world of kitchen design by conducting extensive research and drawing inspiration from a variety of sources. Magazines, websites, social media platforms, and even home improvement programs can provide a wealth of ideas. Create a visual board or scrapbook to collect images, color schemes, textures, and design elements that appeal to you. This process will help you narrow down your style preferences and identify recurring themes to incorporate into your kitchen.

3. Design and layout

Working with a qualified kitchen designer or architect is invaluable at the planning stage. They help you translate your ideas into a functional layout that optimizes your space and workflow. Consider the working triangle in the kitchen, which includes the placement of the sink, stove, and refrigerator, ensuring efficient cooking and food prep. Browse options for open concepts, islands, peninsulas, and other floor plan configurations that fit your lifestyle.

4. Choosing Materials

The materials you choose for a kitchen remodel play a crucial role in achieving the desired look and durability. When choosing countertops, consider durability, maintenance needs, and aesthetics of options like granite, quartz, marble, or butcher block. The wardrobes should fit perfectly into the overall design and offer plenty of storage space. Choose from a variety of finishes, colors and hardware to complement your chosen aesthetic.

5. Hiring Contractors and Obtaining Permits

Depending on the complexity of your remodel, you may need to hire a variety of contractors including plumbers, electricians, carpenters and more. Do your research and get quotes from reputable professionals to ensure quality work. Also, check with your local authorities to see if permits are required for certain aspects of the renovation, such as structural changes or electrical work.

6. Demolition and Preparation

The demolition marks the beginning of a physical transformation. Carefully remove existing furnishings, cupboards, appliances and floor coverings while protecting the recyclables. To ensure safety, properly disconnect the stand at this point. Proper room preparation allows for a smooth remodeling process.

7. Structural changes and installations

If your project requires structural changes, e.g. B. removing walls or enlarging windows, this is the right step. These changes can significantly affect the design and flow of the space. At the same time, install new appliances, plumbing fixtures, lighting fixtures, and outlets according to the design plan.

8. Cabinets and Countertops

The cabinets serve as both a functional storage solution and a striking design element. Whether you choose custom, semi-custom, or storage cabinets, make sure they fit your layout and style. Proper installation is essential for a tidy appearance. Then install the chosen countertops by carefully measuring, cutting and fitting the materials together to create a level surface.

9. Flooring and Finishes

Choose a floor that suits your design vision, considering factors such as durability and ease of maintenance. Whether you choose tile, hardwood, vinyl, or any other material, make sure you install it properly for a flawless finish. Install a backsplash to protect your walls from spills and splashes, adding texture, color and pattern to your space.

10. Finishing touches and inspection

As the renovation draws to a close, focus on the finer details that hold the project together. Add moldings, embellishments and hardware to your cabinets for an elegant look. Before unveiling your new kitchen, do a thorough cleaning to remove dust and dirt. Schedule a final inspection to ensure all work is in compliance with safety regulations and standards.

11. Furnishing and personalization

When the construction dust has settled, it's time to bring your personality into the room. Choose furniture, decorations and accessories that match the theme of your project. Whether you prefer a minimalist, rustic, contemporary or eclectic style, these pieces will add the finishing touch to your kitchen and make it stand out.

12. Celebrate your new kitchen

Once your remodel is complete, take a moment to celebrate the culmination of your hard work and vision. Host a get together, invite friends and family over to dinner, or simply enjoy the joy of your renovated kitchen. This space is now more than a functional space; It's a reflection of your creativity and a testament to your dedication.

Summary

Starting a kitchen remodel takes patience, dedication and a strategic approach. By carefully defining your goals, doing extensive research, working with professionals and making informed decisions at every step, you can transform your kitchen into an oasis of function and beauty. As you cook, gather and make memories in this newly refurbished space, you will find that the satisfying result is more than worth the effort you put in.

Chapter No. 2

Setting Your Renovation Goals: Defining Your Vision

Introducing

The prospect of a kitchen makeover is exciting and promises a refreshed and revitalized space that best suits your needs and style. At the beginning of this journey, setting clear renovation goals and defining your vision are essential steps that influence the entire process. Your kitchen is more than just a functional space; It is a canvas for creativity, a hub for activity and a reflection of your personality. In this guide, we look at the
process to set comprehensive remodeling goals and develop a clear and inspiring vision for your dream kitchen.

1. Assessing your needs and lifestyle

A successful renovation begins with a thorough assessment of how you currently use your kitchen and how you plan to use it in the future. Take time to think about your lifestyle:

Are you passionate about cooking and do you spend a lot of time in the kitchen?
Do you frequently receive guests who need ample seating and a well-organized layout?
Are there particular issues in your current kitchen that make daily tasks difficult?
Is your family growing or changing and need a more functional and flexible space?

2. Identify Weaknesses

Every kitchen has its flaws, and identifying those weaknesses is key to setting effective remodeling goals. Consider the areas where your current kitchen is underperforming:

Not enough counter space for meal prep?
Are your storage solutions inadequate, leading to clutter and clutter?
Do you struggle with low light conditions that affect both ambience and functionality?
Are outdated appliances and accessories reducing the efficiency of your kitchen?

3. Determine your aesthetic preferences

Your kitchen design should fit your personal style and preferences. Explore different design styles and get inspiration to create a mood board that reflects the aesthetic you want. Think about color combinations, materials, textures, and architectural details that match your vision.

4. Prioritization

When setting goals, prioritize them based on their impact on daily life and overall happiness. Consider dividing your priorities into three tiers:

These are non-negotiable issues that significantly affect your kitchen's functionality and comfort.
Medium Priority: These goals improve the overall experience and aesthetics of your kitchen.
Background: These are optional items that are desirable but do not drastically affect the usability of your kitchen.

5. Budget Considerations

Renovation goals must be within budget. Examine the costs in relation to your priorities, including expenses for materials, labor, permits and potential contingencies. Make room for unexpected spend by identifying areas where you want to spend more on higher quality materials or features.

6. Future Vision

Take a moment to envision the transformed space. Imagine the flow of activity, the warmth of natural light and the functionality of well-placed furnishings. Imagine moving smoothly around the kitchen, completing everyday tasks with ease and enjoying the aesthetics of your dreams.

7. Seek Professional Advice

Even if you have a clear vision, seeking professional advice can sharpen your ideas and make your goals achievable. Kitchen designers, architects, and contractors can give you insights into layout optimization, materials, and design considerations that you may not have thought of.

8. Document Your Vision

Create a comprehensive document that captures all aspects of your vision and renovation goals. Add written descriptions, sketches, inspirational images, and any specific design elements you want to include. This document will be a valuable reference for communicating with professionals and making decisions during the renovation process.

Summary

Establishing your renovation goals and defining your vision is the first step that will give you the power and foundation for a successful kitchen remodel. By assessing your needs, troubleshooting, and imagining the potential of your space, you arm yourself with the knowledge and inspiration to complete the remodeling process with confidence. Your kitchen reflects your desires and lifestyle. By setting your goals carefully, you can be assured that the end result of the will live up to your expectations and truly become the centerpiece of your home.

Chapter No. 3

Budgeting for Success: Financial Planning for Your Dream Kitchen

Introduction

A kitchen makeover is a transformative endeavor that promises to breathe new life into your home. However, for the renovation to be successful and stress-free, careful financial planning is the most important thing. By creating a comprehensive budget that takes into account all potential costs, you can approach the remodeling process with confidence and achieve the kitchen of your dreams. In this guide, we'll look at the key aspects of budgeting for a kitchen remodeling project.

1. Assess Your Financial Situation

Start by assessing your financial situation. Take a close look at your savings, available credit, and other potential sources of funding. Know your budget limits and determine how much you are willing to invest in your kitchen remodeling project without jeopardizing your overall financial stability.

2. Creating a realistic budget

Creating a clearly defined budget is the basis of successful financial planning. Find out about the average costs associated with various aspects of a kitchen renovation such as: B. Materials, equipment, labour, permits and design services. Create a detailed budget spreadsheet that details these expenses and includes a contingency fund for unexpected expenses.

3. Prioritize

Prioritize renovations within your budget. Rank your goals in order of importance:

Non-negotiable: Key elements to improve functionality and resolve issues.
Improvements: Improvements to improve aesthetics and overall user experience.
Luxury: Optional features that may be included if your budget allows.

4. Estimating Costs

Research carefully and collect cost estimates from various contractors, suppliers, and vendors. Compare the prices of materials, equipment, devices and services. A clear understanding of costs avoids overpayments and allows you to make more informed decisions.

5. Allow for unforeseen events

Unforeseen challenges often arise during renovations. Set aside an emergency fund, typically around 10-20% of the total budget, to cover any unexpected expenses that may arise during the project. This buffer ensures you are prepared for surprises without jeopardizing your financial plan.

6. Allocate work equipment

Labor costs, including specialty jobs like plumbing, electrical, and plumbing, can have a significant impact on your budget. Receive detailed cost estimates from your contractors and include these expenses in your budget allocation.

7. Consideration of design and aesthetics

Design and aesthetics play a fundamental role in the outcome of the renovation. Allocate funds for design services, custom finishes, and decorative elements that match your vision. Make sure your budget includes the visual impact you want.

8. Finding Financing Opportunities

If your budget doesn't meet your remodeling goals, consider several financing options. Home equity loans, personal loans, or lines of credit can provide the additional funds you need to realize your vision. However, make informed decisions about taking out a loan by considering interest rates and repayment terms.

9. Track Expenses

Keep a careful record of all expenses during the restructuring process. Document bills, invoices and payments to track your spending and monitor any discrepancies. Keeping records like this keeps you in control of your budget.

10. Flexibility and compromises

Remain flexible and open to change when renovating. Certain items may need to be impacted or reprioritized due to unexpected costs or design changes. Get ready to customize your projects without going over your budget.

11. Regular Budget Reviews

Review your budget regularly to see if you're on the right track. Adjustments may be necessary if unexpected costs arise or you decide to make changes to your original plan.

12. Celebrate your investment

Once your kitchen remodel is complete, take the time to celebrate your investment. Host a get-together to showcase your new spaces, invite friends and family over to dinner, and enjoy the results of your budget and renovations.

Summary

Budgeting your kitchen remodel is a strategic process that will help you create the space you love while maintaining financial stability. By assessing your financial situation, creating a realistic budget, and considering contingencies, you'll be well-equipped to handle the complexities of the renovation process. Your well-executed financial plan will not only transform your kitchen, but also give you peace of mind by ensuring your dream space is achievable and sustainable.

Chapter No. 4

Exploring Kitchen Design Styles: From Traditional to Modern

Introduction

The kitchen is much more than a functional space; It's a canvas to express your unique style and personality. Choosing the right design style for your kitchen remodel is an important decision that affects the ambiance, aesthetics and overall feel of the space. From the timeless appeal of traditional designs to the sleek minimalism of modern aesthetics, each style has its own appeal. In this guide, we explore the different kitchen design styles so
can find the perfect combination for your dream kitchen.

1. Traditional kitchen design

Traditional kitchens combine tradition and classic elegance and radiate warmth and friendliness:

Materials: High-quality, natural materials such as wood for cabinets, panels and floors.
Details: Moldings, raised panels and intricate detailing.
Colors: Neutral color palettes with warm tones such as creams, browns and muted whites.
Cabinet fittings: Classic, elaborate fittings with antique or brushed surfaces.
Textures: Layered textures through elements such as tile patches and patterned rugs.
Lighting: sophisticated and decorative lighting such as chandeliers or pendant lights.

2. Transition kitchen design

Transition kitchens strike a balance between classic and contemporary, offering a harmonious combination:

Lines: clean lines and an emphasis on simplicity.
Materials: mixes materials such as wood with elegant tabletops.
Colors: Neutral color palettes, sometimes accented with bold colors or patterns.
Cabinet Design: Cabinets with recessed panels and flat surfaces offer versatility.
Lighting: Flexible lighting options, from modern pendant lights to classic chandeliers.
Furniture: Complements the combination of traditional and modern furniture and decorations.

3. Country Kitchen Design

Country kitchens capture the inviting charm of country life with a touch of nostalgia:

Materials: Reclaimed wood or reclaimed wood for cabinets, floors and exposed beams.
Features: Pre-wash basin and open shelving create a functional yet rustic look.
Colors: Muted, muted color combinations with occasional subtle color accents.
Lighting: Vintage-inspired fixtures like tin can pendants or wrought-iron chandeliers.
A Mixture of Modern and Rustic: A combination of modern appliances with rustic textures and finishes.

Font: Features a stonewashed finish and antique hardware for a lively feel.

4. Modern Kitchen Design

Modern kitchens celebrate clean lines, functionality and contemporary aesthetics:

Simplicity: Clean finishes and an emphasis on open space.
Materials: metal, glass and concrete give it an elegant and modern look.
Colors: monochrome palettes with white, black and gray tones.
Cabinets: Flat panel cabinets with minimal embellishment and concealed hardware.
Lighting: Minimalist, geometric fixtures as artistic focal points.
Technology: technologically advanced devices and intelligent functions to increase efficiency.

5. Contemporary design kitchen

Contemporary kitchens take current design trends into account and are a mix of different styles:

Evolutionary design: Flowing and evolutionary design, inspired by different eras.
Colors and Textures: Vibrant colors and mixed textures, including glossy finishes.
Lighting: Eye-catching lights that add character and drama.
Simplicity and Organization: Clean lines that emphasize organization and functionality.
Balance: A balance between minimalist and decorative elements.
Presentation: Open shelves or display cabinets to display decorative items.

6. Industrial kitchen design

Industrial kitchens draw inspiration from urban aesthetics and functional design:

materials: exposed brick walls, concrete floors and metal details.
Functionality: Useful design that emphasizes practicality.
Colors: Neutral palettes with occasional bright pops of color.
Faucets and Appliances: Elegant looking stainless steel faucets and faucets.

Warehouse: Open shelving and overhead bins for displaying tools and equipment.
Lighting: expressive lights with an industrial character, such as the cage-shaped suspensions.

Contents

Choosing a design style for the kitchen is an artistic journey that allows you to customize every corner of your kitchen. From traditional elegance to modern minimalism, each style offers its own aesthetic that can transform your space into a true reflection of your preferences. By exploring these design styles, you'll gain insight into the elements that interest you, and you'll be better equipped to create a kitchen that not only meets your functional needs, but also exudes beauty and personality.

Chapter No. 5

Crafting a Functional Layout: Maximizing Space Efficiency

Introduction

A kitchen remodel is the perfect opportunity to transform your kitchenette into a functional and efficient center that suits your culinary needs and lifestyle. A well thought-out floor plan is the basis of a successful kitchen and enables smooth operation, sufficient storage space and optimal use of space. In this guide, we explore the art of creating a functional kitchen design that maximizes the use of space and allows you to create a kitchen that not only looks attractive but also fits seamlessly into everyday tasks.

1. Understanding the Kitchen Work Triangle

The concept of the kitchen work triangle is at the heart of effective kitchen design. This triangle connects the three main work areas of the kitchen: the stove, the sink, and the refrigerator. The goal is to create an efficient flow that minimizes unnecessary steps when moving between these areas when preparing and cooking meals.

2. Assess Your Needs and Activities

Before designing your layout, assess your eating habits, family size, and lifestyle:

Cooking Frequency: Do you cook often, or do you prefer quick meals?
Family Dynamics: How Many People Will Use the Kitchen at One Time?
Entertainment: Do you host meetings that require additional counters or seating?
Storage Needs: What kind of storage solutions do you need to store your ingredients, utensils and gadgets?

3. Designing the Layout

Consider several kitchen layout options to find the one that best suits your space and needs:

Kitchen in a Kitchen: Ideal for small spaces, this layout includes parallel countertops and a clear middle ground.
L-Shaped Kitchen: This arrangement creates an L-shape and maximizes corner space for efficient work areas.
U-Shaped Kitchen: By creating a U-shape, this layout puts more workspaces within reach. Kitchen
Open space: the combination of the kitchen with the dining or living room guarantees fluid cooking and social gatherings.
Island or Peninsula Layout: The introduction of an island or peninsula provides additional work space, storage, and often additional seating as well.

4. Prioritize storage solutions

Effective storage is the cornerstone of a functional kitchen. Consider adding:

Deep drawers: ideal for pots, pans and large items.
Sliding Shelves: Better access to items in the base cabinets.
Vertical Storage: Use the space for pans, cutting boards and trays.
Custom Pantry Systems: Streamline storage of dry goods, canned goods and kitchen essentials.

5. Optimize workspaces

Divide your kitchen into separate areas to simplify tasks:

Prep area: near the sink for washing, chopping and preparing meals.
Cooking zone: around the hob for cooking and baking.
Storage Area: Adjacent to refrigerator and pantry for easy access to ingredients and utensils.

6. Good lighting

Good lighting is essential for functionality and atmosphere. Embed:

Task Lights: Brightly illuminate work surfaces so you can focus on tasks.
Ambient lighting: General lighting that provides uniform illumination throughout the room.
Accent Lighting: Highlight design elements like spotlights or open shelving.

7. Focus on ergonomics

Consider ergonomics for user comfort:

Keep frequently used items close at hand to reduce fatigue.
Adjust the height of the table top to your preferred working position.
Make sure there is enough space between your devices and your workspace to allow you to move around comfortably.

8. Traffic Management

Keep traffic flowing smoothly:

Keep main roads clear of obstructions.
Provide enough space for many people to move without clutter.
Guarantees the full opening of cabinet and appliance doors without impeding passage.

9. Get professional advice

When in doubt, consult a kitchen designer or architect for their expertise in optimizing the layout for functionality and aesthetics.

10. Using Design Tools

Use kitchen design software or online tools to view different layouts and experiment with ideas before finalizing the design.

Summary

Creating a functional kitchen layout that maximizes space utilization is an art that balances practicality and aesthetics. By using the work triangle in the kitchen, emphasizing storage solutions, optimizing workspaces and paying attention to ergonomics, you create a kitchen that guarantees even cooking. Whether you choose an L-shaped, U-shaped or open-plan kitchen, focusing on creating a well-designed space will result in a kitchen that is not only visually appealing, but also a pleasure to work with.

Chapter No. 6

Storage Solutions: Organizing Your Kitchen Space

Introducing

An organized kitchen is at the heart of culinary efficiency and a delight for any home cook. When it comes to a kitchen makeover, incorporating clever storage solutions is key to creating a space that not only looks attractive but also functions flawlessly. From ingenious cabinet designs to innovative pantry systems, this comprehensive guide will walk you through countless storage ideas to transform your kitchen into a haven of order and convenience.

1. Maximize your storage space

Pull Out Drawers: Replace traditional shelves with pull out drawers to ensure every corner is accessible and no items get lost in the back.

Lazy Susan: Make efficient use of corner cabinet space with lazy susans that open to allow easy access to cooking utensils and containers.

Vertical Dividers: Equip deep cabinets with vertical dividers to easily organize cutting boards, pans and trays.

Pull-Out Trays: Integrate pull-out trays into small appliance storage cabinets for order and functionality on counters.

2. Efficient Pantry Systems

Adjustable Shelves: Choose adjustable pantry shelves to accommodate different sized products and ensure you don't waste space.

Sliding Baskets: Metal wire sliding baskets can be placed in the pantry for systematic storage of produce, snacks, and packaged products.

DOOR ORGANIZERS: Attach organizers to the inside of your pantry door to store condiments, paper, foil, and other essentials.

Sliding Pantry: When space is at a premium, consider sliding pantry systems that offer deep storage while maintaining accessibility.

3. Creative Drawer Solutions

Utensil Trays: Choose extendable or adjustable utensil trays to match your cutlery and utensil drawers.

Knife Blocks: Choose between built-in knife blocks or magnetic strips to securely organize and store your knives.

Divider Drawers: Create special deep drawer areas for utensils, kitchen appliances and even chopping boards.

Spice Drawer Inserts: Incorporate spice organizers into your drawers to organize your spice collection while keeping it accessible.

4. Clever Shelving Ideas

Floating Shelves: Install floating shelves to display decorative items, cookbooks and commonly used tableware with a touch of style.
Plate Rack: Display your favorite plates and bowls on plate racks to add an elegant aesthetic to your kitchen.
Open Shelves: Combine open shelving with closed cabinets to balance functional storage and tasteful display.

5. Integrated Appliance Storage

Appliance Garage: Create appliance garages with roller doors to hide small appliances like toasters and blenders while maintaining a clean look.
Microwave Drawer: Use the microwave drawer to save countertop space and keep things tidy.
Pull-Out Spice Rack: Install a pull-out spice rack near the stove for quick access to kitchen essentials.

6. Under-Sink Organization

Pull-Out Trash Cans: Place pull-out trash cans and wastebaskets under the sink for a discreet and efficient waste management solution.
Pull Out Shelves: Optimize vertical space under the sink with pull out shelves, ideal for storing cleaning supplies and containers.
Closet Door Caddy: Attach organizers to the inside of closet doors to store cleaning supplies, brushes and more.

7. Island functionality

Built-in storage: Customize your kitchen island with built-in storage such as drawers, shelves and even special bottle holders. Bar seating
: Extend the island's overhang to accommodate bar seating and combine the dining area with functional island storage.
Hidden Trash Can: Effortlessly build a hidden trash can on the island for convenient disposal.

8. Customized solutions

Sliding cabinets: Use the sliding cabinets to organize trays, cutting boards and pans efficiently.
Drawer Dividers: Customize your drawers with dividers to accommodate your specific kitchen tools and utensils, keeping things organized.

Cart: Consider a versatile cart with shelves for extra storage and the flexibility to move it when needed.

Conclusion

A well-organized kitchen is the basis of culinary excellence. By thoughtfully integrating storage solutions like pull out drawers, efficient pantry systems, creative drawer designs and innovative shelving ideas, you can transform your kitchen into a space that maximizes every inch of available space. With built-in appliance storage, under-sink organization, functional islands, and bespoke solutions, you not only get an aesthetically pleasing kitchen, but a seamless productivity hub. Remember that a successful kitchen renovation is not just about looks; It's about creating a comfortable and uncluttered environment that enriches your dining experience and facilitates your daily activities.

Chapter No. 7

Countertop Considerations: Choosing the Perfect Surface

Introduction

The slabs play a fundamental role in the kitchen as they combine functionality and aesthetics. Choosing the right countertop material for your kitchen remodel requires a thorough analysis of durability, maintenance, appearance and budget. This guide will walk you through the basics of choosing the perfect worktop surface, ensuring your decision fits your kitchen needs and design preferences.

1. Material Options

Explore the wide range of worktop materials available, each with their own unique characteristics:

Granite: Renowned for its natural beauty, durability and variety of patterns and colours.
Quartz: Engineered to provide a harmonious combination of natural aesthetics, durability and low maintenance.

Marble: Appreciated for its elegance, although more delicate and requiring careful maintenance.
Solid Surface: non-porous surfaces in various colors that integrate perfectly with washbasins.
Butcher Block: warmth and character of wood that requires regular maintenance.
Concrete: a modern industrial style, customizable in color and finish.

Laminate - practical with a variety of patterns, but less heat resistant.
Stainless steel: modern and hygienic, even if it is prone to scratches and fingerprints.

2. Durability and Care

Choose a countertop that suits your care and lifestyle preferences:

Longevity: Choose quartz and granite for their resistance to stains, scratches and wear.
Moderate Durability: Consider solid surfaces, concrete, and stainless steel for a balance of durability and maintenance.
Regular maintenance: If you want to take the time for proper maintenance, opt for marble or wood countertops.

3. Aesthetics

Harmonizes your favorite worktop with the design of your kitchen:

Classic elegance: granite and marble radiate a timeless charm with their unique grains and patterns.
Modern Sophistication: Quartz and concrete offer an elegant and contemporary aesthetic.

Warmth and Charm: The butcher block and wood give it a warm and rustic look.
Versatile options: Solid surface and laminate worktops are available in many colors and patterns.

4. Choosing colors and patterns

Make sure the worktop you choose matches your kitchen's color palette:

Neutral tones: Choose neutral worktops as a versatile backdrop for a variety of kitchen design accents.
Contrasting Colors: Consider countertops that contrast with cabinets or splash backs for visual impact.
Natural Patterns: Take advantage of the veins and patterns inherent in materials like granite and marble.

5. Budget Considerations

Budget is an important factor when choosing a ceiling:

Affordable Options: Laminate and solid surface ceilings offer affordable choices.
Midrange: Quartz and butcher block countertops combine durability and budget considerations.
Investment Objects: Granite, marble, and concrete countertops may require more investment but offer quality aesthetics.

6. Lifestyle and usage

Evaluate how you use your kitchen and choose a worktop that suits your habits:

Intensive cooking: Go for durability by choosing heat-resistant granite or quartz and knife cuts.
baking enthusiasts: choose marble or butcher block for optimal baking and cooking surfaces.
Fun: Choose countertops with a solid surface to perfectly integrate sinks and create a fluid and entertaining space.

7. Maintenance Requirements

Rate the maintenance procedure you are willing to perform:

Low Maintenance: Quartz, granite, and solid surface countertops generally require minimal maintenance.

Regular Maintenance: Marble and wood countertops require occasional sealing and careful maintenance.

8. Longevity and Investment

Consider the durability of your chosen worktop material and its enduring value:

A Long-Lasting Investment Quality granite, quartz and marble worktops can add value to your home.
Renewable Materials: Wood countertops can be sanded and finished, extending their lifespan.

9. Sample Testing

Before making your final selection, take samples and test them for common cooking processes such as slicing, coloring and heat exposure.

Summary

Choosing the ideal countertop material for your kitchen remodel requires a balance of durability, aesthetics, maintenance and budget. Whether you prefer the natural charm of granite, the modern versatility of quartz, or the warmth of butcher block, each material offers distinctive properties that can enhance both the functionality and visual appeal of your kitchen. By considering factors such as durability, care, color, pattern, budget and lifestyle, you can confidently choose a worktop surface that not only meets your immediate needs but also adds value and aesthetics to your kitchen.

Chapter No. 8

Cabinet Chronicles: Selecting Cabinets for Style and Function

When starting a kitchen remodel, choosing the right furniture is one of the most important decisions you need to make. Cabinets not only contribute to the overall style and aesthetics of your kitchen, but also play an important role in optimizing functionality and storage space. In this guide, we'll take a look at the key points to consider when choosing furniture that seamlessly blends style and function, transforming your kitchen into a truly unique space.

1. Define the style of your kitchen

Before getting into the technical details, take a step back and think about the style you want for your kitchen. The choice of cabinet should be consistent with the overall design concept. Whether you prefer a sleek, modern look, a charming country vibe, a classic, traditional style, or something completely unique, your wardrobe style will set the tone in any room.

2. Door types

Doors are an important visual element in your kitchen. Different door styles evoke different feelings and match different design themes.
Shaker Style: Clean lines and a timeless look that fits well in a variety of settings.
Flat Panel: Modern and minimalist, it offers a sleek and clean look.
Raised Panel: Traditional and elegant, with a sense of depth created by the raised central panel.
Glass Front: Adds a touch of elegance to the presentation of selected items.

 Open Shelf: A trendy option for a more open and airy feel, but with less hidden storage space.

3. Material considerations

The material of furniture doors and frames affects both aesthetics and durability. The most popular are:

hardwood: classic and resistant, it can be stained or painted in different colors.
Plywood: A cheaper alternative to solid wood, which is often used in furniture construction.
MDF: Provides a smooth surface for painted surfaces commonly used for door panels.

Laminate: Very versatile, available in many colors and patterns and easy to clean.

4. Design and functionality

The effective design of a kitchen is above all functionality. Consider the following:

Working triangle: Arrange the sink, stove and refrigerator in a triangle for optimal function.
Storage Solutions: Includes features such as extendable shelves, turntables and deep drawers to maximize storage efficiency.
Island or Peninsula: Consider whether an additional work or living space would enhance the functionality of your kitchen.

5. Hardware and Accessories

Furniture hardware and accessories add style and practicality:

Knobs or Handles: Choose whether you prefer knobs, handles or a combination of both for opening doors and drawers.
Soft-Close Hinges: Create a quieter environment in your kitchen by choosing cabinets with soft-close hinges.
Under Cabinet Lighting: Add function and atmosphere with well-placed lighting.

6. Choice of colors and finishes

The color and finish of the cabinets plays an important role in the overall look of the kitchen:

Neutral tones: Versatile and timeless, neutral colors create a clean and inviting look.
Bold Statements: Consider adding color or a darker shade for a unique and dramatic effect.
tinted vs. Lacquered: Choose stained wood for a natural look or lacquered finishes for a glossy look.

7. Budget Considerations

Finally, match your cabinet selection to your budget:

storage cabinets: Ready and affordable, available in standard sizes and styles.
Semi-Custom Cases: Offer more design flexibility while remaining cost-effective.
Custom Cabinets: Tailored to your needs, but usually the most expensive option.

8. Optimizing Space and Layout

When choosing furniture, optimizing the kitchen layout is key to efficient use of space:

Cabinet Configuration: Choose from low cabinets, wall cabinets and tall cabinets that best suit your storage needs.

corner solutions: Use the corner space efficiently with corner cabinets, turntables or pull-out organizers. Vertical Storage
: Maximize your vertical space with tall cabinets or sideboards in your pantry for storing items not in daily use.

9. Closet Organization

A well-organized kitchen makes cooking and meal prep easier:

Drawer Dividers: Drawer dividers help you organize kitchen utensils, cutlery, and cooking utensils.
Pull Out Trays: Install pull out trays or shelves for easy access to items stored in the back of cabinets.
Spice Racks and Liners: Consider built-in spice racks, utensil covers and tray dividers to keep things organized.

10. Durability and Maintenance

Choose cabinets that will stand the test of time and are easy to maintain:

Quality Construction: Look for cabinets that are solidly constructed, with hardwood elements and well-finished edges.
Easy-to-clean surfaces: Choose easy-to-clean and stain-resistant materials and surfaces.
Durability: Invest in furniture that will last for years, especially if you plan on staying in your home for a long time.

11. Ecological options

If you are interested in sustainability, take a look at our selection of ecological furniture:

Bamboo: a material that renews itself quickly, is durable and offers a distinctive look.
FSC Certified Wood: Look for furniture made from FSC certified wood for responsible sourcing.
Low VOC Finishes: Choose cabinets with low VOC (VOC) finishes to minimize indoor air pollution.

12. Consult a Professional

If you are unsure of what design or layout would work best for your kitchen, consider consulting a professional:

Interior Designer: An interior designer can help you create your Adapt furniture selection to your overall design vision.

Kitchen Designer: A kitchen designer specializes in optimizing kitchen layouts and can suggest cabinet configurations that best suit your space.

13. Visualize Your Choices

Many hardware stores and online platforms offer virtual design tools that you can use to visualize how the various cabinets in your kitchen will look. Use these tools to better understand how your choices fit together.

14. Sampling and Testing

Request furniture samples or visit the showrooms to see and touch the materials before making your final decision. You can also try opening and closing doors and drawers to see if they are working properly and reliably.

15. Expandable flexibility

When choosing your wardrobe, let the future guide you. Will your needs change? Are you thinking of selling your home? Cabinets that balance your current needs with potential future scenarios are a wise investment.

16. Personalization

You can give your kitchen a unique touch by customizing the wall units:

Glass inserts: Choose glass inserts with decorative patterns or frosted glass to add a visual touch.

Cabinet Moldings: Moldings can add an elegant and sophisticated look to your cabinets.

Open Shelf Combinations: Combine closed cabinets with open shelves for a versatile and visually appealing mix.

17. Timeless vs. Trend

Find a balance between trendy elements and timeless options to keep your kitchen elegant for years to come. While trendy colors or hardware are great, make sure your wardrobe basics are classic.

18. Final Measurements

Make sure the measurements are correct before finalizing your wardrobe order. Any measurement errors can lead to costly corrections in the future.

19. Installation Considerations

Whether you hire professionals or do the installation yourself, make sure the installation process is well planned and tailored to your chosen furniture and floor plan.

Remember that the cabinet selection process is both exciting and crucial to your kitchen remodel. When you carefully weigh these extended considerations, you create a kitchen that is not only beautiful but also functional and meets your needs.

Chapter No. 9

Cinks and Faucets: Functional Features with Design Impact

When it comes to kitchen renovations, sinks and faucets are the unsung heroes, combining function with sophisticated design. These elements play a key role in the overall performance and aesthetics of your kitchen space. In this guide, we go over the most important aspects when choosing sinks and faucets that not only provide convenience, but also improve the visual appeal of your kitchen.

1. Sink Styles and Materials

Sinks are available in a variety of styles and materials, each with its own unique aesthetic and benefits:

Undermount Sinks: These sleek and modern sinks are used for an intriguing look under the counter installed.
Countertop Sinks: Also called drop-in sinks, they are easy to install and offer a classic look.
Farmhouse
sinks: With an exposed front apron, these sinks have a charming, rustic vibe.
Materials: Choose stainless steel for a modern look, fireclay for strength and a classic look, or composites for a wide range of colors and stain resistance.

2. Sink Configuration and Dimensions

When choosing your sink configuration and dimensions, consider your workflow and kitchen space:

Single Bowl: Provides ample uninterrupted sink space for larger items.
Dual Bowl: Provides separation for tasks such as washing and rinsing, or preparing and cleaning food.
Triple Bowl: Perfect for multitasking, with separate areas for different tasks.

Size : Choose a size that suits your kitchen needs without taking up counter space.

3. Faucet functions

faucets have evolved and offer many functional and practical features:

Pull-out or pull-out spray: Provides flexibility when washing dishes and cleaning the sink.
Touchless Technology: Operate the faucet with your hand, reducing the spread of germs.
bow raised against. Low Arc: High arc faucets offer more room for taller pots and pans, while low arc faucets offer a slimmer look.

4. Faucet Design and Finish

faucets have a significant impact on the aesthetics of the kitchen:

Finish Options: Choose from a variety of finishes such as chrome, brushed nickel, stainless steel, matte black and more.
Matching Hardware: Match the faucet finish to other hardware in your kitchen for a cohesive look.

5. Compatibility and Installation

Make sure the sink and faucet you choose are compatible with your countertop and cabinet configuration:

Number of Holes: Check the number of holes required for installing the faucet are required and ensure your sink or countertop has the appropriate holes Correct number.
Top Plate: Consider a top plate to cover additional flush holes if your chosen faucet requires fewer holes.

6. Consider Ergonomics

Ergonomics matter when choosing your sink and faucet:

Sink Depth: A deeper sink can minimize splashes and make washing large items easier.
Faucet Handle Position: Choose a faucet with a handle that feels comfortable and natural to you.

7. Water Efficiency

Choose high-efficiency faucets to save water:

Flow: Look for low-flow faucets to reduce water consumption without sacrificing performance.
Aerator: The faucet aerator mixes air with water, reducing water consumption while maintaining adequate pressure.

8. Care and cleaning

When choosing materials for sinks and faucets, pay attention to ease of maintenance:

Stain resistance: Choose materials that are dirt-repellent and easy to clean.

anti-fingerprint: Some surfaces, such as B. brushed nickel and matte black, are less prone to fingerprints.

9. Additional accessories

Furnish your washbasin with more functionality and style:

Soap dispenser: Keep your worktop tidy with the integrated soap dispenser.
Sink Grates: Protect your sink surface from dents and scratches with the sink grates.

10. Budget Considerations

Balance desired features with budget:

Investment Characteristics: Quality sinks and faucets can provide long-term value, making the initial investment worthwhile.
Affordable Options: Affordable options are available that still offer durability and style.

11. Long-Term Vision

Choose sink and faucet styles that fit your long-term design vision and make sure they remain relevant even as you decide to update other parts of your kitchen.

12. Practicality and aesthetics

Find a balance between practicality and aesthetics: a sink and faucet must meet your functional needs while enhancing the overall look of your kitchen.

13. Professional Installation

For a sleek, professional look, consider having your sink and faucet installed by a qualified plumber or contractor.

14. Visual Models

Use design tools or software to create visual models of how your chosen sink and faucet will look in your kitchen before making your final decision.

15. Periodic Maintenance

After installation, the sink and faucet should be maintained according to the manufacturer's instructions to ensure optimal life and performance.

When you carefully consider these broad aspects when choosing sinks and faucets, you not only increase the functionality of your kitchen, but also create an aesthetically pleasing space that fits well with your lifestyle. Remember that these items are the most important parts of your kitchen. So choose them wisely to ensure they serve you well for many years to come.

Chapter No. 10

Kitchen Appliances Unveiled: From Essentials to Innovations

Embarking on a kitchen renovation journey immerses you in a world of kitchen appliances where functionality, practicality and technological advances meet. In this guide, we take a comprehensive look at kitchen appliances - from essential tools to cutting-edge innovations - to help you make informed choices that suit your culinary needs and design aspirations.

1. Refrigerators: Not just cooling

Refrigerators have become versatile storage solutions with multiple functions:

French doors: offer large shelves and a freezer below for easy access.
Side-by-Side: Provides equal vertical sections for fresh and frozen products.
Smart Fridges: Equipped with touchscreens, apps and cameras for inventory management and recipe suggestions.

2. Ranges: From traditional to highly technological

ranges are available in different styles to suit different cooking preferences:

Gas ranges: Loved by chefs for precise temperature control.
Electric ovens: equipped with smooth and easy-to-clean plates.
Induction cookers: use electromagnetic fields for fast and energy-efficient cooking.

3. Ovens: standard for convection.

Conventional ovens: standard cooking and roasting.
Convection Ovens: Use fans to distribute heat evenly for faster, more even cooking.
Steam Ovens: Combine heat and steam for healthier cooking and better texture.

4. Dishwashers: Effortless cleaning

Modern dishwashers have become powerful and feature-rich:

Energy Efficient: Look for Energy Star certified models to save on your electricity bills.

Quiet operation : Consider low decibel models for a quiet kitchen environment.
Smart Dishwasher: Some models can be controlled remotely via a smartphone app.

5. Microwave Ovens: Versatile Helpers

Microwave ovens aren't just for heating anymore:

Long Range Microwave Ovens: Save countertop space by installing them above the oven.
Microwave drawer : ideally integrated in base cabinets.
Combined Convection Microwave: Also serves as a second cooking oven.

6. Hoods: Aesthetic and practical

hoods provide ventilation and style:

ventilation performance: choose a hood that effectively evacuates smoke and odors. Design
Element : Consider a range hood that complements the aesthetics of your kitchen.

7. Coffee machines: individual preparations

Coffee lovers can enjoy coffee tailored to their individual needs:

filter coffee machines: classic and simple for daily preparation.

Disposable egg : perfect for quick and personalized cups.
Coffee Machines: For preparing delicious coffee drinks at home.

8.Smart Appliances: The Technological Revolution in the Kitchen

Technology has entered kitchen appliances:

Smart Fridges: View recipes, calendars and more on built-in displays. Ovens
with WiFi connection: monitor preheating and cooking remotely.
voice-activated devices: Control your devices with virtual assistants like Amazon Alexa or
Google Assistant.

9. Specialty appliances: Expand your culinary journey of discovery

Enhance your kitchen with special appliances:

Wine coolers: Store and present your wine collection at optimal temperatures.
sous vide devices: precise cooking by immersion in water.
built-in steam oven: preserves nutrients and flavors while cooking.

10. Appliance surfaces: Aesthetic harmony

appliance surfaces contribute to the visual harmony of your kitchen:

stainless steel: Elegant, modern and fingerprint-proof. Black
Stainless Steel: Offers a dark and sophisticated alternative.
Custom Panels: Seamlessly blend devices with furniture for a unified look.

11. Energy efficiency: environmental considerations

Choose devices with energy-saving features:

Energy Star certification: indicates high energy efficiency.
Inverter Technology: Used in refrigerators and microwave ovens, it regulates output to save energy.

12. Budget

The cost of household appliances varies greatly. So plan your budget carefully:

Prioritize the things that matter most: Invest more in powerful appliances like refrigerators and stoves.
Setting Realistic Expectations: Balancing Features with Budget Constraints.

13.Durability and Guarantee

Choose trusted brands that are known for their durability and look for comprehensive guarantees to protect your investment.

14. Sizing Right

Make sure your new appliances will fit your kitchen perfectly by taking accurate measurements before purchasing.

15. User Reviews and Research

Browse online reviews and user experiences to get an overview of the performance and features of the devices you are considering.

16. Future-proof

Consider devices that adapt to possible lifestyle changes, e.g. B. a growing family or changing cooking habits.

17. Intuitive Interfaces

Choose devices with intuitive controls and interfaces that make them easy to use and understand.

18. Care and cleaning

Choose appliances with surfaces that are easy to clean and maintain to keep your kitchen spotless.

19. Personalized Cooking Styles

Choose the appliances that suit your cooking habits, whether you're an experienced cook or someone who prefers quick and easy meals.

20. Professional Advice

Consult appliance specialists or kitchen planners to ensure you are making decisions that meet your remodeling goals.

By analyzing these detailed kitchen appliance considerations, you will acquire the knowledge needed to create a kitchen workspace that is not only efficient, but also integrates perfectly with the overall design vision. From traditional necessities to futuristic innovations, every appliance choice contributes to the heart of your home: the kitchen.

Chapter No. 11

Lighting Your Kitchen: Creating Ambiance and Functionality

A well-done kitchen renovation is about more than just choosing the right furniture and countertops. Lighting plays a key role in transforming the kitchen into a space that harmoniously combines ambience and functionality. By strategically planning your kitchen lighting, you can improve the overall aesthetic, create a comfortable atmosphere and ensure optimal performance. This guide covers the different aspects of lighting during a kitchen renovation, detailing how to give the perfect balance of mood and function.

1. Types of Furnishings:

Choosing the right type of furnishings is crucial to achieve the desired effect in your kitchen. There are three main types of lighting:

Mood lighting: Provides general lighting so that the entire kitchen is well lit. Recessed spotlights, chandeliers and pendant lights are popular options for ambient lighting.

Task lighting: Task lighting is designed to provide adequate lighting for specific work areas such as counters, ranges and sinks. Under-cabinet lighting, track lighting and dimmable pendant lights are commonly used as task lighting.

Accent Lighting: Accent lighting adds drama and depth to your kitchen by emphasizing architectural features, decorative elements or focal points. This can be achieved with spotlights, light strips and even LED strips.

2. Stackable Lighting:

To create a balance between ambient, task and accent lighting, different types of luminaires need to be stacked. Layering allows you to customize lighting for different activities and moods. For example, if you're cooking while you're cooking, you might want bright lighting for activities, while at a party, you might prefer dim ambient lighting.

3. Color temperature:

The color temperature of the lights has a major impact on the overall appearance of the kitchen. Warm white (approx. 2700K to 3000K) creates a warm, inviting atmosphere, while cool white (approx. 4000K to 5000K) is more energetic and business-friendly. Consider using color temperature combinations to achieve just the right balance.

4. Smart Lighting Solutions:

Incorporating smart lighting technology can add a new dimension to your kitchen remodel. With smart lighting, you can control intensity, color and even the lighting schedule via a smartphone app or voice commands. This flexibility enhances both functionality and ambience, allowing you to easily adapt the lighting to different scenarios.

5. Pendant lights:

Pendant lights are not only functional, but also serve as decorative elements. They can be hung over kitchen islands, dining tables or counters to provide functional lighting while adding a touch of style. Choosing pendant lights to complement your kitchen's design aesthetic can enhance the overall look.

6. Base cabinet lighting:

The base cabinet lighting is a practical accessory for illuminating work areas on the counter. Prevents shadows and provides focused light when preparing meals. Popular options for this are LED strips or light discs.

7. Dimmers and Controls:

Installing dimmers and lighting controls gives you the ability to adjust the brightness to suit your needs. Dimming the light can create a softer atmosphere for casual gatherings or intimate dinners.

8. Incorporate natural light:

Maximize the use of natural light in your kitchen whenever possible. Consider placing windows and using reflective surfaces to enhance the effects of sunlight. Natural light not only improves the overall aesthetic, but also contributes to a healthier and more energetic environment.

9. Niche lighting:

Niche lighting involves installing lights in a niche or shelf, creating a soft, indirect light that will add a touch of elegance to your kitchen. This type of lighting can be used to highlight architectural features such as ceiling beams or crown molding, enhancing the overall look of a space.

10. Ceiling Lighting:

Ceiling lights such as chandeliers and recessed lights can be used for mood lighting as well as decorative lighting. Chandeliers in particular can add a sense of grandeur and style to your kitchen by becoming the focal point that unifies the entire design.

11. Positioning of the lighting:

The positioning of the lights is crucial to achieve the desired effect. For example, if you're installing pendant lights over an island, make sure they're hanging at the right height to provide enough light for the task without blocking the view or causing glare. If you use recessed lights for ambient lighting, you should consider their placement and position to avoid uneven lighting.

12. Color and material issues:

The colors and materials used in your kitchen can affect the reflection and absorption of light. Lighter surfaces tend to reflect more light, making the space appear brighter and more open. Darker surfaces, on the other hand, can absorb more light, creating a more intimate and warm atmosphere. Consider how the lighting you choose will interact with the color palette and materials in your kitchen.

13. Hanging Set:

For a unique and artistic lighting solution, consider a hanging set. Instead of using a single pendant light, group multiple lamps of different shapes, sizes, and heights in one place. This layout can act as a focal point and add a dynamic visual element to your kitchen.

14. Lighting level control:

The ability to independently control different lighting levels can improve both functionality and ambience. For example, you may want to keep the overhead lights dim during hospitality to create a cozy atmosphere, but leave the task lights bright for meal prep. This level of control allows you to adapt the lighting to different situations.

15. Lighting for an open-plan kitchen:

If your kitchen is part of an open-plan living space, consider how the lighting design will affect adjacent areas. A consistent lighting style and color temperature can create a smooth transition between spaces, enhancing overall visual harmony.

16. Energy Efficiency:

Choose energy efficient lighting solutions to reduce power consumption. For example, LED bulbs last longer, use less energy and generate less heat than traditional incandescent bulbs. This choice not only saves you money, but also helps make your home greener.

17. Lighting and Security:

Bring light to areas where security is important. For example, stairways and potentially dangerous corners can benefit from well-placed lighting to prevent accidents and improve visibility.

18. Professional Advice:

While there are many online resources that can help you, the advice of a professional lighting designer can provide invaluable information tailored to your specific space and needs. They will help you create a lighting plan that takes into account your kitchen layout, your personal preferences and the atmosphere you want.

In summary, lighting is a multifaceted aspect of kitchen renovation that not only affects the aesthetics but also the functionality and comfort of the space. By considering different types of lighting, their locations, color temperatures, and controls, you can create a well-lit kitchen that enables a variety of tasks and enhances the overall cooking, dining, and socializing experience.

Chapter No. 12

Flooring Foundations: Durability and Design underfoot

When embarking on a kitchen remodel, choosing the right flooring is one of the most important decisions you need to make. The kitchen is a high-traffic area with frequent spills, dropped utensils, and constant foot traffic. Your floor needs to strike a balance between durability and design to ensure it can handle the demands of a busy kitchen while also contributing to the overall aesthetic. This guide addresses the considerations when choosing a kitchen floor that offers durability and style.

1. Material Choices:

There are many flooring materials available, each with their own benefits and considerations: Tile : Ceramic or porcelain tile is highly durable and resistant to stains, moisture and heat. Available in a wide range of colors, patterns and textures, they allow for diverse design aesthetics. However, joint ducts can be prone to dirt build-up and require maintenance.

Parquet: Hardwood gives your kitchen warmth and timeless elegance. However, it is important to choose a hardwood that is strong and resistant to moisture and possible splashes. Regular sealing and care is essential to keep the wood looking its best.

Vinyl Flooring: Vinyl is a versatile and economical option. It comes in the form of slabs, slabs or planks and can mimic the look of natural materials such as wood or stone. Vinyl is water resistant, easy to clean, and soft to the touch.

Laminate Flooring: Like vinyl, laminate can mimic the appearance of hardwood or tile. It's durable and inexpensive, but may not be as moisture resistant as other options.

Natural stone floors: Materials such as granite, marble and limestone provide a high-quality, luxurious look. However, they can be more delicate and porous and need to be sealed regularly to prevent staining.

2. Durability and maintenance:

Given the intensive use of your kitchen, durability is essential. Choose floor materials that are stain, scratch and moisture resistant. An important factor is also the ease of cleaning the floor. The splash-proof and easy-to-clean surface makes maintenance easier.

3. Comfort Underfoot:

While durability is important, comfort should not be neglected. Kitchens are places where we spend a lot of time on our feet and on the move. Choosing a flooring material that offers some cushioning and is not too harsh can reduce fatigue and discomfort.

4. Style and aesthetics:

Your kitchen floor influences the overall appearance of your room. It should complement the color scheme, cabinets, countertops and other design elements. For example, a sleek, modern kitchen might feature shiny tiles or concrete floors, while a country-style kitchen might look pretty with aged hardwood or patterned tiles.

5. Consistent Design Flow:

Consider the layout of your home and how your kitchen floor will interact with adjacent areas. When your kitchen is part of an open floor plan, choosing a flooring material that complements the rest of the space is essential for a smooth transition.

6. Waterproof and Durable:

With the likelihood of spills and water-related accidents occurring in the kitchen, a waterproof or waterproof floor would be a practical choice. Some flooring options, such as luxury vinyl planks, are fully waterproof, making them a great solution for kitchens.

7. Preparing the subfloor:

The nature of the subfloor is crucial to the durability of the chosen floor. Make sure the sub-floor is level, dry and free of any problems that could affect the installation and performance of the floor material.

8. Professional installation:

Regardless of the floor material selected, we recommend professional installation. Proper installation ensures that the floor adheres well, is firmly bonded and can withstand the rigors of everyday use.

9. Green Options:

If you care about the environment, explore green flooring like bamboo, cork, or reclaimed wood. These materials are renewable and have a lower environmental impact than some traditional floor coverings.

10. Consider traffic patterns:

Analyzing traffic patterns in your kitchen can help you choose your flooring. Identify key passageways and high-traffic areas, e.g. B. the space in front of the sink, the stove and the refrigerator. Choose a more resilient floor in these areas to avoid wear and tear over time.

11. Slip resistance and safety:

Kitchen floors can become slippery, especially when wet. Safety comes first, so floor coverings with good slip resistance are paramount. Some tile and vinyl options feature a textured surface that improves traction and reduces the risk of accidents.

12. Trendy vs. Timeless:

While it's tempting to choose flooring options based on current trends, there are also long-term implications to consider. Trends come and go, but your floor is likely to stay in place for many years to come. If you opt for a classic and timeless look, you can be sure that your kitchen will retain its charm even with changing design trends.

13. Visual enhancement and comfort:

The size of your kitchen can influence the choice of floor covering. A lighter floor can visually enlarge a small kitchen, thereby making it more open and spacious. On the other hand, a darker floor can create a warm and cozy atmosphere, perfect for larger kitchens or kitchens with high ceilings.

14. Flooring transition:

If your kitchen opens up to other rooms with different flooring materials, consider how the transition should be designed. Thresholds or transitions can help create a smooth transition between spaces, improve overall aesthetics, and prevent trip hazards.

In summary, a subfloor for a kitchen renovation requires a careful balance of aesthetics, durability and practicality. By considering traffic patterns, safety considerations, durability, budget and personal preference, you can make an informed decision that will improve the functionality and appearance of your kitchen. Remember that a good floor covering not only adds value to your home, but also serves as the backdrop for countless memories in your culinary paradise.

Chapter No. 13

Backsplash Brilliance: Elevating Your Kitchen Walls

When it comes to kitchen remodeling, a kitchen splashback is a small but eye-catching piece that can dramatically change the look of your space. Functional and aesthetically pleasing, a well-designed kitchen splashback not only protects the walls from splatters and stains, but also adds personality and style to your kitchen. In this guide, we'll delve into the nuances of selecting and installing a splashback baseboard that will add luster to your kitchen walls.

1. Variety of Materials:

Backsplashes are available in a variety of materials, each offering a unique aesthetic and functionality:

Ceramic or Porcelain Tile: These tiles are valued for their versatility and durability. They come in a variety of shapes, sizes, colors, and patterns to accommodate virtually any design theme.

Glass tiles: Glass tiles give your kitchen an elegant and modern touch. They reflect light to create the illusion of space and come in a variety of colors and finishes.

Natural Stone Tiles: Materials such as marble, travertine and slate create an organic and luxurious look. Each type of stone has its own unique patterns and color variations that add depth to your kitchen design.

Metal Tiles: Tiles made of stainless steel, copper, and other metals can create an industrial or modern flair. They are extremely heat and moisture resistant and can serve as eye catchers.

Subway Tiles: Timeless and classic, subway tiles are hugely popular due to their simple yet versatile looks. They go great with a variety of design styles from traditional to contemporary.

Mosaic Tiles: Mosaic tiles are made up of small elements that create intricate patterns. They allow for creative designs and can be made from a variety of materials such as glass, stone and ceramics.

2. Matching the design aesthetic:

The screen should fit into the overall design of your kitchen. Whether your kitchen has a rustic, farmhouse feel, a sleek modern look, or somewhere in between, a kitchen splashback should help create a cohesive design story.

3. Play with color and pattern:

The color and pattern of the kitchen splashback can complement or contrast with other kitchen elements such as cabinets and countertops. Think about the visual effect you want to achieve, whether it's a subtle background or an eye-catching element.

4. Visual extension or usability:

As with the floor covering, the choice of back covering can influence the perceived size of your kitchen. Light colors on the splashbacks can make a small kitchen look more spacious, while darker tones can create a cozier, more intimate atmosphere.

5. Texture and Dimension:

The texture adds depth and interest to your backsplash. From textured tiles to materials like hardboard or embossed sheet metal, incorporating textures can add a tangible, vibrant quality to your kitchen walls.

6. Choose your grout:

The color of grout you choose can make a world of difference in the look of your backsplash. A contrasting grout can emphasize a tile pattern, while a matching grout can provide a more uniform look.

7. Functionality and maintenance:

Practicality is key when it comes to mudguards. It should be easy to clean and resistant to stains, as it can splash and spill. Choosing materials with smooth surfaces and minimal seams can make maintenance hassle-free.

8. Height Considerations:

Decide how high you want the tailgate to extend. While the standard height is between the tabletop and the upper cabinets, you can opt for a full-length, anti-glare screen that extends to the ceiling for a dramatic effect.

9. Statement to the contrary:

 Fineness Determine whether the backsplash should be an eye-catcher or an unobtrusive background. A bold and eye-catching splashback can become the star of your kitchen, while a more understated design lets other elements shine.

10. Inlet and Fittings Integration:

plan to integrate inlets and fittings into a backsplash design. Decide whether you want your outlets to be visually striking or stand out, and consider under-cabinet lighting or pot-fill batteries if necessary.

11. DIY or Professional Installation:

The complexity of the material and design of the back cover can make the difference between doing the installation yourself or hiring professionals. Intricate designs or delicate materials may require a skilled hand to ensure flawless execution.

12. Visual Continuity:

If your kitchen is part of an open space, consider how the backsplash design will affect adjacent areas. Visual continuity contributes to a cohesive and harmonious living environment.

13. Care and durability:

Choose a splash guard material that suits your lifestyle. While some materials require regular sealing or maintenance, others are more durable and require minimal maintenance.

In summary, the backsplash is a canvas that allows you to express your personal style while serving a practical function. By carefully selecting materials, colors, patterns and textures, you can create a splashback that will add glamor to your kitchen walls. A carefully selected and well-made kitchen splashback enhances the aesthetics of your kitchen and becomes a distinctive element that arouses the admiration of all visitors.

Chapter No. 14

Harmonizing Colors: Designing a Cohesive Kitchen Palette

Color is a powerful tool in kitchen design that can create atmosphere, influence the perception of space and create a sense of harmony. When it comes to a kitchen renovation, it is important to choose a color palette that not only reflects your personal style, but also works well with the different decorative elements. This guide looks at the art of harmoniously mixing colors in the kitchen for a visually pleasing and balanced result.

1. Define the base color:

First select a base color that will serve as the basis for your kitchen palette. This color is likely to be used on larger areas such as walls, cabinets, and countertops. Choose a shade that fits your overall design vision and desired mood.

2. Complementary Colors:

Complementary colors are the opposite colors on the color wheel. By using complementary colors you can create visual contrast and vibrancy in your kitchen. For example, a combination of blue furniture with orange accents can create a dynamic and energetic atmosphere.

3. Analogous colors:

Analogous colors lie side by side on the color wheel. Using analogous colors can result in a more harmonious and relaxing color palette. For example, a combination of shades of green, blue, and turquoise can create a calm, cohesive impression.

4. Neutral Anchors:

Neutrals such as white, gray and beige provide a versatile backdrop that can balance bolder colors and prevent spaces from becoming cluttered. Neutral tones also contribute to a timeless and elegant aesthetic.

5. Accent Colors:

Accent colors add character and interest to your kitchen. They are generally used in smaller doses, such as in accessories, decorative items, or even on a single wall. Accent colors can breathe life into your design and emphasize certain features.

6. Consistency Between Elements:

Make sure your color scheme is consistent between the different elements in your kitchen. The color of the cabinet should match the countertop, back wall, floor and even the appliances.

Consistency creates a sense of unity and avoids visual chaos.

7. Consider the lighting:

The lighting in your kitchen can affect the appearance of colors. Natural light and various types of artificial lighting can change the perceived color of a surface. Test the colors you choose under different lighting conditions to ensure they look as intended.

8. Create a visual flow:

Think about how the colors you choose guide the eye through the room. The smooth transition of colors from one area to another creates a sense of continuity and visual flow, helping to create a harmonious environment.

9. Variety of textures and finishes:

Different textures and finishes in the selected color palette can add depth and visual attractiveness. For example, a combination of matte and glossy surfaces can avoid monotony and enhance your design.

10. Balance of warm and cool tones:

A balance of warm and cool tones can create a sense of balance in your kitchen. Warm colors like red and yellow can make you feel more comfortable, while cool colors like blue and green can have a calming effect.

11. Try small samples:

Before deciding on a color scheme, get small samples of selected colors and materials. See how they interact with each other in the lighting conditions in your kitchen. This way you avoid unpleasant surprises when everything is installed.

12. Consult the color wheel:

The color wheel can be an invaluable tool in understanding how different colors relate to each other. It can help you visualize the relationships between colors and help you make decisions.

13. Personal preference and functionality:

Remember that the choice of color must match your personal preference and the expected functionality of your kitchen. If you are attracted to certain colors or have specific needs (e.g. a calming atmosphere in a busy house), prioritize these factors when deciding on a color palette.

In summary, when renovating a kitchen, color matching is a complex process that involves choosing a base color, matching complementary and similar hues, and maintaining consistency between elements. By choosing your color scheme carefully and considering factors like lighting, texture and personal preference, you can create a kitchen that is not only aesthetically pleasing but also welcoming and harmonious. A well-coordinated color scheme can bring your kitchen to life, transforming it into a space that reflects your style and enriches your everyday experience.

Chapter No. 15

Eco-Friendly Choices: Sustainable Options for Your Renovation

As environmental considerations become more important, incorporating green choices into your kitchen remodel can have a significant positive impact. By choosing sustainable materials, energy efficient appliances and eco-friendly design practices, you can create a kitchen that not only looks stylish but also minimizes the environmental impact. This guide explores different ways to make eco-friendly choices when renovating your kitchen, creating a greener and more sustainable living space.

1. Sustainable Materials:

Choose materials that are responsibly sourced and have a lower environmental impact. Look for certifications such as Forest Stewardship Council (FSC) for wood products or Cradle to Cradle (C2C) for products intended to be recycled or reused. Bamboo, reclaimed wood, recycled glass, and recycled metal are examples of sustainable materials to consider for cabinets, countertops, and flooring.

2. Low VOC paints:

Volatile Organic Compounds (VOCs) are chemicals found in many paints, varnishes and glues that can emit harmful fumes into the air. Choose coatings with low or no VOC levels to improve indoor air quality and reduce exposure to potentially harmful toxins.

3. Energy saving devices:

Energy saving devices not only reduce energy consumption, but also the bills. Look for devices with the ENERGY STAR label, which indicates they meet the US Environmental Protection Agency's (EPA) stringent energy efficiency guidelines.

4. LED lighting:

LED (Light Emitting Diode) lighting is very energy efficient and lasts longer than traditional light bulbs. Use LED bulbs for kitchen fixtures, including under cabinet lights, pendant lights, and recessed lights.

5. Water-saving faucets:

Choose water-saving faucets and faucets to save water. Look for faucets with the WaterSense label, which indicates they meet EPA criteria for water performance and efficiency.

6. Reclaimed and Recycled Materials:

Reclaimed and recycled materials contribute to a unique and eco-friendly kitchen design. Consider using reclaimed wood for the shelves, reclaimed tile for the back wall, or recycled materials for the decorative pieces.

7. Recycled content:

Choose products made from recycled materials. Countertops made from recycled glass, tiles made from recycled materials and furniture made from recycled wood can help reduce the need for new resources.

8. Eco-friendly worktops:

Explore options such as recycled glass worktops, sustainably sourced butcher blocks or composite worktops made from recycled materials such as fiberglass and bamboo.

9Effective space planning:

Effective space planning can reduce the need for excess materials and resources. Optimize your kitchen layout to minimize wasted space, which can also lead to more functional and organized kitchen spaces.

10. Composting and Recycling Stations:

Include designated areas for composting and recycling in your kitchen design. This promotes environmentally friendly waste disposal and makes it easier to develop sustainable habits.

11. Local Sourcing:

Choose local materials and products whenever possible. This reduces the carbon footprint of transport and supports the local economy.

12. Durability and Longevity:

Invest in quality, durable materials and craftsmanship so your kitchen will last for years. By choosing materials that do not need to be replaced frequently, overall waste is reduced.

13.Donate and Reuse:

If you're replacing old furniture, appliances or lighting fixtures, consider donating them to charities or reusing them in other parts of your home. As a result, the items do not end up in landfill and can be reused.

14. Eco-friendly paint:

Choose paints with low VOC content and minimal environmental impact. Some brands offer paint shops that are specifically designed to protect the environment.

15. Sustainable flooring:

Consider options like bamboo, cork or reclaimed wood for your kitchen flooring. These materials are renewable and have a lower environmental impact than traditional hardwoods.

Overall, making green choices when renovating your kitchen is part of a sustainable and responsible approach to design and living. By choosing sustainable materials, energy efficient appliances and conscious design practices, you can create a kitchen that is not only aesthetically pleasing but also environmentally friendly. Your organic cuisine becomes an expression of your commitment to a greener future and, for example, to a sustainable lifestyle.

Chapter No. 16

Navigating Plumbing and Electrical Upgrades

Introduction

Renovating a kitchen is a multifaceted project that requires attention to detail, creativity and an understanding of the technical aspects. Key themes include plumbing and electrical improvements that underpin the functionality and efficiency of the kitchen space. Effectively managing these updates requires a holistic approach, from initial planning to implementing changes and ensuring compliance.

Planning and design

Working with design professionals

Bringing in the expertise of a kitchen designer or architect is invaluable at the planning stage. They can help you translate your ideas into a functional design by considering factors like your work triangle, storage solutions, and overall aesthetics. Integrating plumbing and electrical requirements early in this design minimizes potential later conflicts.

Assessment of Existing Systems

A thorough assessment of existing plumbing and electrical systems is essential. Understanding the strengths and limitations of your existing setup will help you decide what to upgrade, replace, or reconfigure. This assessment will also help you estimate the scope of work required and potential costs.

Plumbing Improvements

Plumbing Improvements

Modern kitchens require an efficient water supply for cooking, cleaning and using appliances. Upgrading water pipes with a larger diameter or increasing the water pressure with booster pumps can improve the functionality of the kitchen. Consider factors like water hardness and filtration systems to improve water quality.

Drainage and Ventilation

Proper drainage and ventilation are essential in the kitchen. It's important to upgrade or relocate drains to accommodate new sinks, dishwashers, or additional appliances. Good ventilation prevents the formation of unpleasant odors and mold. The vent pipes may need to be adapted to the new arrangement.

Notes Appliance

Each kitchen appliance has specific plumbing requirements. Dishwashers, refrigerators with ice cube makers and water dispensers and pot fillers require special connections. Working with a plumber ensures your plumbing infrastructure is in place to seamlessly integrate these devices.

Gas Lines and Appliances

If your kitchen uses gas for cooking, you may need to upgrade your gas lines and connections if you move stoves or add gas appliances. In order to avoid leakage and danger, gas pipelines must comply with safety rules and regulations.

Upgrade Your Electrical System

Strengthen Your Electrical System

The modern kitchen is filled with electrical needs, from high power appliances to various gadgets. Assessing the performance of your existing panel is critical. If that's not enough, upgrading to a higher amperage panel can prevent overloading and circuit shutdowns.

Outlets and GFCIs

Strategically placed outlets are essential for powering small devices, charging stations and more. Residual current device (GFCI) outlets are an essential safety feature, especially near water sources. An electrician can determine the optimal location of outlets and ensure their compliance.

Lighting design

Kitchen lighting has both functional and aesthetic purposes. Functional lighting for the kitchen, mood lighting for the dining room and lighting to accentuate design elements require careful planning. Different types of lighting require different wiring configurations.

Energy efficiency and smart technology

The use of lighting, energy efficient appliances and smart technology can increase the sustainability and comfort of your kitchen. Wiring smart devices, lighting controls, and home automation systems may require special attention when upgrading your electrical system.

Career Guide

Hiring Licensed Contractors

Qualified professionals including plumbers and electricians are an essential part of a successful renovation. Their knowledge ensures that updates are not only visually appealing, but also secure and compliant. Correct installation avoids problems such as leaks, electrical hazards or insufficient power supply.

Obtaining Permits and Inspections

Permits are required for major plumbing and electrical work in most jurisdictions. This process involves submitting plans and conducting checks at various stages to ensure work is in compliance with safety standards and building codes. Compliance ensures the well-being of your family.

Summary A kitchen remodel with plumbing and electrical upgrades is a major undertaking that requires careful planning and execution. By working with design professionals and hiring licensed contractors, you can successfully navigate the complexities of these upgrades. The result will be a kitchen that perfectly combines functionality, aesthetics and safety, enhancing your living space and enriching your daily life.

Chapter No. 17

Working with Professionals: Contractors and Designers

Beginning a kitchen remodeling project can be exciting and daunting at the same time. The heart of any home, the kitchen is a multifunctional space that requires careful planning and execution. Working with experienced professionals, including contractors and designers, is essential for a successful renovation. Their expertise not only helps you realize your vision, but also ensures that your project is delivered successfully, on time and within budget. In this guide, we look at the critical role contractors and specifiers play in a kitchen renovation and provide insights into effective ways to work with them.

1. Contractors: the basis of a successful renovation

Contractors are the backbone of any renovation project, tasked with turning design ideas into tangible reality. This is why working with contractors is so important:

Knowledge and experience: Qualified contractors bring years of experience to the table, so they are well equipped to deal with the various challenges that can arise during the remodeling process.

Project Management: Contractors oversee the entire renovation process, coordinating various operations, planning activities and ensuring that the project goes according to plan.

Budget Management: Contractors help you stay on budget by creating accurate cost estimates, sourcing materials at the best prices, and avoiding costly mistakes.

Quality of Workmanship: The use of reputable contractors ensures the use of quality materials and workmanship, resulting in a durable and aesthetically pleasing kitchen.

Communication: Effective communication with the contractor is essential. Be clear about your expectations, timelines, and any specific elements of the project you want to include.

2. Designers: creating functional and aesthetic spaces

Designers play a fundamental role in creating a kitchen that is not only visually appealing but also highly functional. Here's why working with a designer is valuable:

Space Optimization: Designers attach great importance to space planning, ensuring that every square inch of your kitchen is used efficiently. They take into account traffic flow, work areas and storage solutions.

Aesthetics: Designers will help you choose the colors, materials, furnishings and finishes that suit your design preferences and the overall aesthetic of your home.

Innovative Ideas: Designers bring fresh perspectives and innovative ideas to enhance the overall kitchen design.

Coordination: Designers work closely with contractors to ensure that the design concept flows seamlessly into the finished project. This collaboration minimizes potential conflicts and ensures a consistent outcome.

Personalization: The designer adapts the design to your specific needs, lifestyle and preferences to create a kitchen that is perfect for you.

Collaborative Process: Working with a designer is a collaborative process. Be open to their suggestions, share your ideas and work together to improve the design concept.

3. Finding the right specialists

Finding the right contractors and planners for your kitchen remodeling is an important step that can significantly affect the outcome of your project. Here's how:

Search: Start researching local contractors and designers. Look for reputable companies with a proven track record of kitchen remodeling. Read reviews, ask friends or family for recommendations, and browse their portfolios to get a glimpse of their work.

Interviews: After narrowing down your options, schedule interviews with potential contractors and designers. This is your chance to discuss your project, ask questions and gauge understanding of your vision.

References: Check contractor references such as licenses, insurance and certifications. In the case of designers, their education, experience and any professional relationships must be taken into account.

References: Ask for references from previous customers. Contact these references to ask about their experience working with a contractor or designer and the quality of their work.

Budget Considerations: Explain your budget clearly to the contractor and designer. A realistic budget forms the basis of their recommendations and ensures that the project is financially manageable.

4. Collaborative Design Process

Working together with the contractor and the designer is essential to a successful renovation:

Concept Development: Work closely with the designer to develop a design concept that fits your preferences, lifestyle and that of matches the functionality you need. in your kitchen.

Material Selection: A designer can guide you through the material selection process and help you select durable and visually appealing options that fit your budget.

Technical Details: The contractor and designer work together on technical details such as electrical and plumbing plans to ensure project feasibility and regulatory compliance.

Regular communication: Maintain regular communication with the two specialists throughout the project. This helps resolve any issues quickly and ensures everyone is on the same page.

5. Coping with change and challenges

Unexpected challenges can arise during a reorganization. Contractors and designers play a role in managing these changes:

Flexibility: Be prepared for unexpected issues such as hidden engineering issues or design changes. A flexible approach and open communication with both professionals will help you overcome these challenges.

Problem Solving: Contractors and planners know how to solve problems. Rely on their expertise to find solutions to unforeseen challenges while keeping your project goals in mind.

Budget Adjustments: Sometimes changes can affect the budget. Work with the contractor and planner to understand the financial implications of any changes and make informed decisions.

6. Project Completion

When a remodeling project comes to an end, there are a few final steps to ensure its success:

Quality Control: Review the completed work closely with the contractor and designer. Remove any current inconsistencies or fixes that require your attention.

Documentation: Ensure all aspects of the remediation including design plans, contracts, warranties and invoices are properly documented for future reference.

Feedback: Provide constructive feedback to the contractor and designer. Your contribution can help them improve their services and improve their future projects.

In summary, a successful kitchen renovation is based on the collaboration between entrepreneurs and designers. Their combined expertise, from initial design concept to final touches, will ensure your kitchen remodel meets both your functional needs and your aesthetic desires. If you encourage clear communication, remain flexible and rely on professional advice, you are well on your way to enjoying the kitchen of your dreams.

Chapter No. 18

DIY vs. Professional Renovation: Pros and Cons

A kitchen remodel is an extensive undertaking that requires careful thought, whether it's a do-it-yourself project or hiring professionals to do the work. Each approach has its own benefits and challenges. In this guide, we'll go over the pros and cons of renovating your kitchen yourself and having it remodeled professionally so you can make an informed decision.

DIY Kitchen Remodeling:

Benefits:

Save Money: DIY projects can potentially save you money on labor costs because you don't have to hire contractors or designers.

A Sense of Accomplishment: Successfully completing a DIY renovation can be extremely rewarding and boost your confidence in your home improvement projects.

Design Control: You have complete control over the design and decision-making process and can personalize every aspect of your kitchen.

Flexibility: You can work at your own pace and on your own schedule, which can be an advantage when you are pressed for time.

Cons:

Limited Expertise: DIY projects require a certain level of skill and knowledge. If you are inexperienced, you may struggle with complex tasks such as electricity, plumbing, or structural changes.

Time-consuming: Do-it-yourself renovations often take longer, especially if you have other commitments. Delays can result in an extended absence from a functioning kitchen.

Quality problems: without specialist knowledge, the quality of the workmanship and the materials used may not meet the desired standard and the sustainability of the renovation is at risk.

Potential Errors: DIY projects are error-prone, which can result in additional costs for correcting errors or redoing the work.

Benefits:

Expertise: Professionals bring years of experience and expertise to the project, ensuring quality finish and compliance with building codes.

Efficiency: Contractors and planners are adept at managing the schedule and coordinating various aspects of the project, resulting in a more efficient remodeling process.

Design Assistance: Designers can provide creative insight, innovative ideas and expert advice to create a functional and visually appealing kitchen.

Better Results: Professional renovations often result in a tidy, cohesive and aesthetic result that adds value to your home.

Cons:

Higher Cost: Hiring specialists incurs labor and design costs that could increase the overall cost of the rebuild.

Less Customization: While designers may consider your preferences, some decisions can be influenced by experience, which can compromise your vision.

Less Control: You can have less direct control over day-to-day decisions and project progress by relying more on professionals.

Communication Challenges: Effective communication with professionals is essential. Misunderstandings or incorrect interpretations can lead to unsatisfactory results.

Question:

The decision to renovate the kitchen yourself or to hire specialists depends on your level of knowledge, the time available, the budget and the desired result. If you are confident in your abilities and have time to devote to the project, a do-it-yourself approach may be worthwhile. However, if you are looking for a quality, efficient and professionally designed renovation, working with experienced contractors and designers is your best bet. Before makes a decision, carefully assess your priorities and resources, and remember that whichever path you choose, clear planning and efficient execution are essential to a successful kitchen remodel.

Chapter No. 19

Permits and Building Codes: Navigating Legal Requirements

When tackling a kitchen remodeling project, it's important to familiarize yourself with building permits and regulations to ensure the project is not only done correctly, but also complies with local codes. Building permits and regulations are in place to ensure the safety, structural integrity and quality of the renovation. In this guide, we delve deeper into the importance of building permits and regulations when renovating a kitchen and show you how to effectively manage these legal requirements.

1. Construction:

Safety: Building permits and regulations are primarily concerned with the safety of property owners. Residents and adjacent properties. They ensure that the facility meets safety standards to prevent accidents and hazards.

Quality: Building code compliance ensures your renovation is of high quality and meets established standards. This will help you avoid potential problems in the future.

Property Value: A properly approved and compliant renovation can add value to your property. Buyers are more willing to invest in homes with well-done and documented renovations.

Legal Consequences: Failure to comply with building permits and regulations can result in fines, project delays and even the need to remove sub-standard work.

2. Learn about the licensing process:

Research: First, check the licensing requirements in your region. Check with your local building authority to see what permits are required for your particular renovation.

Documentation: Prepare the required documentation, including plans, drawings and specifications, as required by the local building authority. These documents are reviewed to ensure compliance.

Application: Submit an application for admission with the required documents. There may be a fee for the application process, which varies depending on the extent of the renovation.

Review and Approval: The Building Department will review your application and documentation for compliance with building codes. This process ensures that the refurbishment meets the safety and structural requirements.

Permit Grant: Once approved, you will receive the necessary permits to begin the renovation. Make sure these permits are in place and available during the construction process.

3. Building Code Compliance:

Design and Construction: Work closely with the contractor and designer to ensure the design and construction processes comply with local building codes. This includes factors such as structural changes, electrical work, plumbing and materials used.

Inspections: Building inspectors conduct inspections at various stages of renovation to ensure compliance. These inspections often occur after milestones such as construction, electrical, and plumbing work.

Changes: If changes are required based on inspection feedback, these must be addressed immediately to ensure the update is smooth and compliant.

4. Call Professional Advice:

Contractors and Designers: Experienced contractors and designers familiar with permitting processes and building codes. Their expertise can help ensure your remodeling goes to plan from start to finish.

Architects and Engineers: For more complex projects, hiring architects and civil engineers can provide a further assurance of compliance and quality.

Question:

Building permits and regulations are important aspects of any kitchen remodeling project. They guarantee the safety, quality and legality of refurbishments while protecting the value of your property. Navigating the permitting process, complying with building codes and seeking professional advice when needed will help you efficiently navigate the complex landscape of regulatory requirements. In this way, you can carry out a kitchen renovation that not only meets your aesthetic requirements, but also meets the highest standards of safety and quality.

Chapter No. 20

Preparing for Renovation: Demolition and Site Readiness

Before the excitement of renovating your kitchen can begin, it's important to prepare the space for future changes. The first steps, including demolition and site preparation, lay the foundation for a successful rehabilitation. In this guide, we'll cover the key steps required to prepare your kitchen for the remodel, including demolishing, clearing the site, and preparing the space for the upcoming remodel.

1. Demolition: Paving the way for change

Safety First: Start by keeping everyone involved safe. Use appropriate protective clothing such as gloves, goggles and dust masks. Close electrical circuits and water sources to avoid accidents.

Demolition Plan: Work with a contractor or planner to create a demolition plan. This plan should list items to be removed such as cabinets, counters, floors, and appliances.

Careful Disassembly: Start by disconnecting and removing devices. Then systematically remove cabinets, counters and other furniture. Be careful not to damage the surrounding areas, they will remain intact.

Material disposal: Responsible disposal of waste. Some materials may be recyclable while others may require proper disposal according to local regulations.

2. Readiness for construction: Preparation for the next phase

Site inspection: After demolition, the condition of the remaining structural elements, walls and floors must be assessed. Fix any issues that may have occurred during the demolition process.

Structural Adjustments: If the renovation involves structural changes such as removing or adding walls, work closely with contractors and engineers to ensure the changes are made safely and in accordance with regulations.

Utilities and Utilities: Plan any changes or upgrades to utilities such as plumbing, electrical, and HVAC. Coordinate with specialists to ensure necessary changes are made.

Temporary Kitchen Equipment: Your kitchen will likely be out of use during the renovations. Consider setting up a temporary kitchen in another part of the house to ensure you have access to the necessary appliances and space to prepare meals.

3. Ground cleaning: Ground preparation for the construction

Basic cleaning: After the demolition and the structural adjustment, a basic cleaning of the room should be carried out. Remove dirt, dust, and any remaining materials to provide a clean canvas for the next step.

Soil Protection: When a renovation involves replacing the floor, steps must be taken to protect the existing floors during the construction process to prevent damage.

Contains dust and dirt - use plastic wrap to separate build area from other parts of house. This keeps dust and dirt out and minimizes its impact on the rest of your living space.

Storage of New Materials: If new materials have been delivered, ensure that dedicated storage is available for contractors but does not impede the progress of the remediation.

Inquiry:

The prep phase of a kitchen renovation, which includes demolition, site preparation, and land clearing, is a crucial step before the construction phase. Careful planning, adherence to safety protocols, and effective communication with professionals will ensure this transition goes smoothly. By making space, customizing the building, and creating a clean, organized environment, you lay the foundation for a successful renovation.
's meticulous site preparation contributes to your design desires and ensures a smooth transition to building and remodeling your kitchen space.

9 7 9 8 8 5 8 7 8 5 9 6 5